Butterfly in th

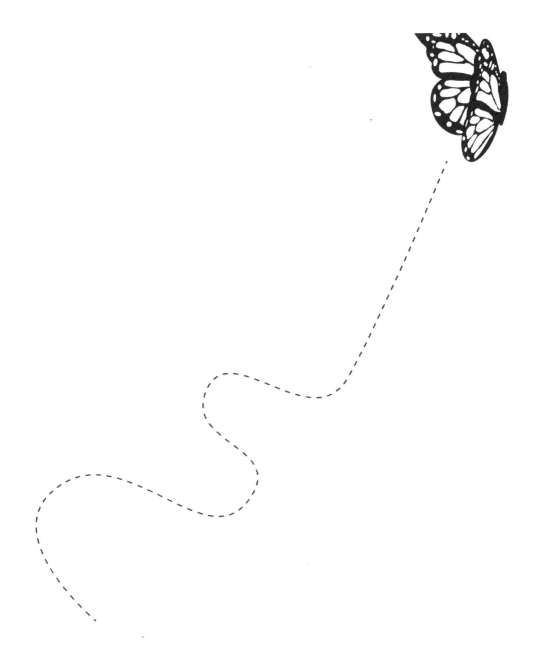

Butterfly in the Reine

Written by:
Jennifer Lauren Accius

Illustrated by:
Don Beamon Jr.

www.reinexrebelle.com

Butterfly in the Reine

© 2017 by Jennifer Accius
All rights reserved.

ISBN: 1533466203
ISBN-13: 9781533466204
Library of Congress Control Number: 2017906212
LCCN Imprint Name: West Palm Beach, FL

Contents

Acknowledgments...............5

i............6

ii.........26

iii.........65

iv.........85

Acknowledgements:
February 6, 2017—10:49 p.m.

To every person I've ever met,
every person I've ever been,
every person who ever was,
for taking part in my being,
I thank you.

i

June 26, 2012—7:53 p.m.

I want to believe that it's only distance
that keeps our hearts imprisoned,
that limits our pure love from blossoming.
The last few seasons
were some of the coldest winters.
I've been holding my breath waiting for spring.
My cheeks are beginning to turn purple.

July 4, 2012—11:00 a.m.

Cheeks black from streaks of mascara.
A big hat shades the sunshine,
and a black veil masks my bloodshot eyes.
Standing in a puddle of tears,
I've cried for your love over time,
wearing my finest little black dress
so that your last memory of me will be the best.
I've got a bottle filled with gasoline to set fire to our love.
There is no point burying
bittersweet memories
that haunt me in my dreams.
One last kiss from your lips will turn my heart to stone.
I won't risk this being the end of me;
the thought will have to do.

July 16, 2012—4:40 p.m.

Big blue sea,
wash over me.
Cleanse my soul of all bad things
so that the only thing left is positivity.
Big blue sea, how you've shown me things far beyond the surface
of what the rest of the world has to offer me.
Big blue sea, I'd explore your depth until the death of me.
The deeper I go, the more I feel close.
Big blue sea, swimming seems just like flying.
You make me feel as though I've grown wings.
My body weightless,
I feel free,
like I can conquer anything.
There is nothing I adore more than the sound
of the waves crashing against the shore.
Serenity.

July 29, 2012—8:24 p.m.

I want to lose myself in a glass of something strong,
just as long as memories of you,
promise to meet me at the bottom.
In my mind, we dance to a never-ending love song.
I follow your lead;
this dance is the most beautiful thing I've seen.
All alone, just us two,
I whisper all the reasons I love you.
And you smile, hold me closer,
because you've known all the while.

August 10, 2012—9:56 p.m.

Good-bye, Austin.
I've loved you in ways
you couldn't comprehend
and were afraid to accept.
It breaks my heart,
but I am not broken.
I've lost you before.
This stint hurts more,
but I am stronger than ever.
Tears fall on my pillow,
and for the millionth time,
you are the reason.
My pride won't allow me to
admit
how brokenhearted I am
or ever harbor any malice toward you.
Karma will take its course.

August 30, 2012—7:42 p.m.

I'll lace my kisses
with a slight hint of good-bye.
It's time we say farewell.
There is no longer a need to try
and salvage something
that is destined to die.
Your hands addicted to
the arch of my back,
length of my neck.
The way my legs seem to be a journey
always takes you on a trip.
My body like a mannequin
that you love to get wrapped up in.

September 9, 2012—4:00 p.m.

Twinkle in his gaze
whenever he lays his eyes on me,
in an instant I can see
his heart smile
and simultaneously break
when he sees my face.
It's like wishing on a star religiously
for dreams that seem so far away.
How blood like this
found its way to my fingertips,
I'm always puzzled with.
Killed his hopes
and didn't notice it.
Came to the realization that there isn't a point
in wasting time if he wasn't the one.
So, I continue this journey in search
of who I can be the moon for, and he my sun.
On the path,
I'm reminded of my past,
hearts I've broken
that insist on revisiting me.
I end up doing more damage to them unknowingly
as I try and find the one that is truly for me.

September 16, 2012—9:54 p.m.

I guess I know how Alice felt in Wonderland—
a beautiful, whimsical world,
so intriguing yet so hard to understand.
Numb to reality, so everything is surreal.
In and out of consciousness,
never holding on to anything
long enough for your heart to feel.
Veins tapped out on love,
a drug once faithful that has turned out to be
your heart's worst enemy.
A fool in the eyes of society,
forced to face insanity alone.

November 17, 2012—12:40 p.m.

Awakened from my slumber,
a rare feeling comes over me.
My bed feels foreign,
as though I don't belong in it.
I can't help but feel like
I'm supposed to be in someone's arms right now,
specifically, his.
In my heart, I feel like he needs me,
that wherever he is,
his heart has sent a message to mine.
With all of my being, I want to be where he is.
I know I should have my head resting on his chest,
our legs intertwined,
his fingers tracing my bare skin.
No words necessary.
No mind chatter.
We'll just fall asleep to the 808 of our heartbeats.
I am now awake with this seemingly magnetic force pulling me.
This isn't where I'm supposed to be.
I feel it;
he needs me.

December 6, 2012—2:28 p.m.

Out of sight, out of mind.
Out of sight, out of mind.
If I erase you from my vision,
promise you won't haunt my memory.
I don't want to be reminded that you aren't mine.
Your presence took my breath away;
your absence made me suffocate.

December 18, 2012—5:15–5:28 a.m.

Like a kid enjoying a bike ride,
I make my way through life,
first traveling to familiar places.
Slowly and curiously riding to places I've never been
in hopes of seeing and experiencing new adventures.
Sometimes going too deep into the unknown, afraid,
panic threatens to creep into my heart.
Just when the mystery of newness feels as though it overwhelms me,
I see something familiar—a tree maybe—that reminds me I'm not too
far from home.
And I find my way back to where I feel I belong,
until I'm moved to travel outside my comfort zone
and discover something new once more.
Being in your presence is my piece of familiarity,
reminds me that I am home,
and inspires me to explore new terrain.
Your love makes me feel like this.

January 1, 2013—7:26 p.m.

Don't Want to Miss a Thing

I find myself trying to silence
these loud thoughts in my head—screaming words of doubt.
Uncertainty trying to seduce me with thoughts
that what I feel for you isn't real
or won't last or matter to make a difference.
I listen to songs similar to how I'm feeling,
seeking some reassurance in the lyrics.
My "logical" mind throws these thoughts to the forefront
in hopes of protecting me from the thing I seem to fear most—
heartache.
Although I've been there before
and made it out on the other side,
heartbreak isn't anything anyone wants to revisit or go through again.
But I refuse to allow myself to be so afraid that I take no action
and always wonder, *What if*.
I pray and ask God every day to help me better understand this
situation.
Give me the strength to pull through and see the lesson in it all.
Music doesn't stop the mind chatter—neither do reading or attempts
at distracting myself.
So, all I want to do is fall asleep,
because maybe then I can see your smiling face,
and I will stop questioning our love.
Because when you smile,
I know that what I feel is real, and rare.
Hoping I see you in my sweet dreams.

February 4, 2013—2:04 a.m.

I'm convinced on nights I wake up like this,
from peaceful slumber abruptly,
that somewhere you need me.
I can feel you tossing and turning as you sleep.
Nights like this, to restore tranquility,
I know all you need of me is to crawl into your bed
with open arms, fingers gently caressing your body.
Lips leaving behind a trail of precious kisses
on the softest parts of your cheek that journey
to your neck, collarbone, and chest.
I'm convinced this will help you rest in bliss.
I can feel that you need me—my touch, the warmth of my love,
whispers of lullabies, and confessions of complete devotion.

February 25, 2013—9:23 p.m.

I can't see your beauty when my eyes are filled with tears,
so why must you make me cry, love?
I can't see the end, but I'm in love with what's presently before me.
The moment is all we've got, so why not make it beautiful?
Paint unforgettable pleasant scenes on the walls of our memories
to remind us on rainy days that life will be okay.

March 29, 2013

You've got a heart as loud as lions;
why let your voice be tamed?

April 2, 2013—11:22 a.m.

Tear-filled eyes tend to hide your beauty,
so why must you make me cry, love?
Neatly stitched my heart back together,
dusted it off, and wasn't sure whether it was fully functional,
but still blindly put it in your hands.
Hands are made to hold, so promise me you won't let go.
I won't let go, I won't let go, I'll never let go.
Like Rose said to Jack, "I'll never let go."
I can't promise to be perfect;
even the most beautiful rose has thorns.

April 10, 2013—10:36 p.m.

It was fun until it wasn't anymore.
Loving you feels the same as a kid riding a carousel.
At first, it's intriguing,
whimsical even.
The warmth of happiness consumes you.
Serenaded by the melodies,
going up and down while spinning,
it feels like flying.
Eyes shut,
hair dancing in the wind,
the cool air tickling your skin,
nothing feels as good as this could.
Nothing can substitute.

Butterfly in the Reine
April 13, 2013—3:00 a.m.

Nightmare on La Reine's Street

It's 3:00 a.m.
I just woke from a nightmare
of someone else's lips and tongue journeying my neck.
I woke up in a cold sweat,
my hand violently rubbing away the unfamiliar feeling.
As if through my slumber, somewhere my dream and reality meet,
his tongue traces my neck,
but it feels nowhere near as sweet.
Our first days of learning one another
after experiencing kisses that brought out passion
I never knew existed inside me,
your lips, on one particular night,
out of curiosity,
decide to discover the rest of my body.
You begin to explore,
your hands tracing all parts of my skin
and caressing the parts you like most. Your fingertips, like magic,
make me feel as though I am made of the finest silk.
A moist trail of kisses
and a few soft nibbles find their way to my left ear.
Your attention turns to my neck, and it's as though you,
ardently lost in an uncharted beautiful city,
somehow stumbled upon a street you knew.
Like your lips had been unknowingly lost for a little over two decades
of my whole existence and finally found themselves at home once more.
This city
belonged to you;
you knew it like the back of your hand,
and it showed as you began to kiss my neck with a foreign
but oddly familiar passion
that from then on became my spot,
our favorite spot to visit
and for you to kiss on my entire body.
When we saw an early end,
after months of forgetting memories,
new lovers had stumbled on that street
and kissed me softly but not quite as sweet.

Butterfly in the Reine

Their caresses not as gentle,
no Houdini fingertips,
my skin just soft skin,
no longer silk.
Even though it wasn't the same,
soon it became easier to fight the urge to call them your name.
And one day altogether,
it no longer threatened to
leave my lips in the middle of a kiss delivered to
a man that wasn't you.
Months go by, and this becomes easier and easier to do,
until the day we meet again.
Your return to the street that had belonged to you
was like just yesterday had been our last rendezvous.
My lungs by now have been breathing air for
close to a quarter century,
and no one else has ever made me feel as alive.
We began to learn each other again.
I welcomed the return of my homey-lover-friend.
My heart,
still haunted by the last unpleasant departure,
reluctantly welcomed you back in.
We haven't spoken in a few days now,
and I was beginning to tell myself I was okay with losing you a second time,
since I had gotten through the first just fine.
My heart fighting with my brain to forget thoughts of you.
But now there aren't only memories;
there are also fingerprints that you left behind
sporadically on my body,
not to mention tattooed initials on my heart.
It'll be much more difficult to forget you.
I know I can do it;
I'm just not sure where to start,
especially because it's 3:00 a.m., and the thought of giving myself to
someone else is as horrifying as a nightmare.
Wake me from this nightmare.

ii

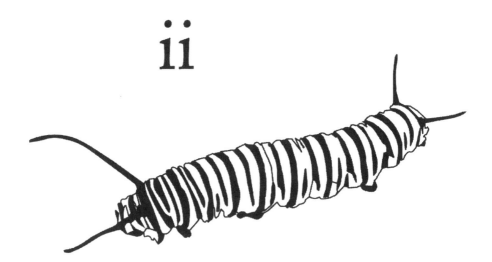

May 8, 2013—10:32 p.m.

Letters to Le Roi

Some days, I wish I could make the world spin a little slower. Time escapes me. It feels like just yesterday that I was a carefree kid playing on a playground at recess. Everyone seemed so genuinely happy then, no need for pretending. If there was sadness, other people actually cared about brightening your day. These days, though, most people pass strangers without a smile or even saying hello. Imagine what that person's day might be like, how much a smile doesn't hurt to give and would help the person on the receiving end. I promise to always greet you with a smile, to make every day feel just as beautiful as the first day. I promise to kiss away all of your sadness, forever and always.

Infinitely yours,
La Reine

May 23, 2013—11:57 p.m.

My dearest Roi,

Some days my heart is as heavy as a ton of bricks. I feel like the world demands so much of me. And because I've been both blessed and seemingly cursed with a big heart, I give all I can. Lately, there hasn't been much left of me. The little that remains I'm sure you'll find to be more than enough. I promise to remain strong and give selflessly and to love with an open heart.

Infinitely yours,
La Reine

Butterfly in the Reine

June 25, 2013—4:29 p.m.

Could it be?
I have stumbled upon something
I've thought was just a figment of my imagination—pure love
in such a jaded nation.
A miracle it seems—that two hearts
that have lost wars
and endured shattered dreams
could meet and in each other find peace
in what seems to be such a graceless age.
Neither of them is afraid to be exposed,
free-falling and allowing their story to unfold
without hesitation or false expectations.
Just focused on the light that still remains
from their darkest nights spent
when they were alone with their pain,
no urge to feel ashamed
completely in the nude.
I've had my fair share of upsets.
You've had disappointments too.
All that has happened led me to you.
And it all starts to make sense.
No need to play pretend,
I gladly open up my heart
when you knock,
and I let you in.

August 4, 2013—1:42 a.m.

I remember that as the tears fell from my eyes that night, I thought to myself, *I can't wait until I forget this moment.* I couldn't wait for the hurt I felt in that moment to be a distant memory. I'd never felt anything like it. My heart had endured enough hurt from the one person I'd done nothing but love selflessly. It was like a fooled-me-twice moment, when you think, *Shame on me for falling for the same thing again.* That moment felt as though it went on forever. Right then, I decided to let go of what no longer served my greater good. Early this morning, while everyone else was asleep, I stumbled upon a tiny scar on my heart, once a gaping hole that seemed like it would never stop bleeding, and I smiled. Honor yourself and be brave enough to let go of something/someone that no longer serves you. Do not be a martyr. Do not be a masochist. Do not romanticize pain. Love shouldn't hurt. As soon as you let go of what isn't right for you, there is room for what is meant to make your heart sing. No pain lasts forever; this too shall pass. Love yourself enough to let go.

Butterfly in the Reine
September 8, 2013—3:00 a.m.

My heart knew
long before my brain.
A faint whisper
of the words, *I love you*
flood my mind,
threatening to jump
from the tip of my tongue
and out of my lips
way before the time appropriate.
Frozen,
still,
like a statue,
I gaze at you
and lose my breath,
my spirit moved
by your beautiful mind.
It was as though our souls
that seemed to be
aimlessly wandering the earth,
two halves,
in that second
became whole,
intertwined.
Like
I'd finally come across the treasure,
unbeknownst to me,
I'd spent my whole life trying to find.
My heart recollected you
from previous lifetimes.
I've found you once more,
and now I remember.
In the beginning of time,
your name was Adam
and mine Eve.
It was from your rib that God created me.
I ate the apple
out of pure curiosity,
tarnishing the paradise we shared.
The regret killed me,
although our love remained.

Butterfly in the Reine
Thousands of years pass.
My name Cleopatra,
yours Mark Antony.
Our love was forbidden,
misunderstood.
We took our own lives
before our enemies could.
Fast forward to the roaring twenties,
during the Harlem renaissance.
I was the daughter of an Italian mobster,
and you were a musician
who played the blues.
I'd sneak to a café uptown after school,
and it was there
I first laid eyes on you.
I'd watch you play your bass with great care.
I loved you in secret,
the way I loved rhythm and blues.
Only in my mind could we have an affair.
In those days,
I wasn't so brave.
Eventually,
the memory of you was buried with me
in my grave.
I found you again.
This time we were introduced through a mutual friend.
At Woodstock, on our blanket, you sat next to me.
I came to see Janis;
you were a fan of Jimi.
We fell in love at that festival,
only for those few days.
At the end, we parted ways,
and I always prayed that you'd remember me.
Remember me,
walking around campus aimlessly,
parked on a bench,
acoustic held close
and carefully in your arms.
I spotted you,
enthralled by you.
My pride wouldn't let me
pass your being by—no, not this time.

Butterfly in the Reine
We engaged in small talk,
as strangers do.
We then went back to our lives,
while every so often, we
passed each other
like two ships in the night.
Four years passed.
I stumbled and fell for you again.
Invited to a house party by a friend,
confused running into you,
the feeling was mutual.
We talked under the moonlight,
no details spared.
We have shared
and built so much.
Who knew such beauty could be birthed
from a mustard seed of love?
Tornado tempers threatened
what we carefully created together.
We became enemies.
During turbulent weather,
we found shelter in each other.
On days that our love was on life support,
recovery was no guarantee.
It all started to get to me.
Love has died and been resurrected
in the same lifetime.
Bittersweet memories
comfort and plague us
as we embark on this new journey.
No one said it would be easy
or rainbows and butterflies.
Love after heartbreak,
searching for truth
to anchor on to
when I look into your eyes.
May this new path be glorious;
may we hold each other close;
may we be an example,
if only for ourselves.
May we be victorious
after we've failed.

Butterfly in the Reine
It is our divine design to be.
We've got something worth keeping,
reincarnating to come together again.
Let's make this life a masterpiece.

July 1, 2013—8:45 p.m.

My beloved Roi,

You challenge me to be better than I've ever been while honoring my past self. This is such a refreshing and defining moment in my life. A ride that isn't familiar but does not lack intrigue. I am ready and willing. I feel that this will demand a lot of me—even better. I am glad to have a partner along for the journey.

Love,
La Reine

June 2, 2013—4:39 p.m.

Close your eyes, baby love.
Don't it feel like we're soaring,
like we've found a prize?
Our hearts journey the sky.
That's the way it feels whenever you're by my side.

December 6, 2013—8:42 p.m.

Are we falling apart,
or am I running away?
Her anxious heart throbs for the
answer to the call of love.

January 19, 2014—12:19 p.m.

There are many ways to recognize when I feel love for a person, place, or thing. The most common way by far is when my heart begins to beat slower. My eyes water because I don't want to miss a thing by blinking. My stomach feels like butterflies are performing the most exquisite ballet, and I almost forget to breathe. It's like everything stops moving, and a smile makes its way to my lips. Like my soul has hushed all the noise to stop and say thank you. I can never predict when a moment like this will occur, but when it does, I know I've stumbled across love in one of its many forms once more. For this, I am grateful.

April 10, 2014—10:49 p.m.

I used to hope the day would come for me to meet your mother.
That is when I'd know you were serious.
Four years of back and forth,
entertaining one another.
I was curious
about what she was like,
prepared interesting conversation.
We'd laugh over dinner.
She'd smile pridefully,
knowing her son found a winner.
All I'd seen were pictures on a computer screen.
She's got such a big, beautiful smile,
with kind eyes.
Accepting of everyone—that's the type of person she looked like.
I could imagine the type of woman you'd bring home to meet her:
cultured, intelligent, multilingual, demure, studying something
interesting in school.
She is not me.
But still, I was hopeful.
I knew that I would win your mother with my charm
if given the chance.
Sway her with my smile, and
tell her about my many talents.
Impress her with my manners, and
show that I've got great core values.
You never took me to meet her,
so I'll always wonder.

July 10, 2014—8:48 p.m.
Day 2

My sweetest Roi,

I've grown to really miss your presence. Forty-eight hours haven't even passed. I have been doing a lot of self-reflection. I've come to realize through the span of a year that somewhere I got lost. I lost sight of what an immense love we share. I've been wrapped up in my circumstances. I forgot the sleepless, tear-filled nights I endured with a bruised heart, praying that God would align me with someone who dances with my soul the way you effortlessly do. Thank you for your presence, for your patience, and for your everlasting love. Most of all, thank you for reminding me of how wonderful you are. I love you for all eternity.

Your love,
La Reine

July 11, 2014—7:19 p.m.
Day 3

Roi,

I miss you more each time I wake up alone. You waking me up with your plush kisses has me spoiled and really wishing for them when you're away. I will make a point to kiss your lips when mine beg for it. There must be more kisses! Got out of our home to spend quality best-friend time. Doing just what you said, getting out and having fun! You were right; it is what I needed.

Love,
Jenn la Reine

July 12, 2014—8:36 p.m.
Day 4

Lovely Roi,

I crave your tenderness. No one has ever taken the time to handle me with care the way that you do. After a day of running around, my body and spirit needs TLC that only you can give. And I can only imagine what your body craves of my touch. I'm making sure your homecoming will be beyond special.

Forever more,

La Reine

July 12, 2014—6:25 p.m.
Day 5

My love Roi,

I'm feeling like myself for the first time in a while. God is so good. Anna has a weird way of always reeling me back. My worries and circumstances were getting the best of me, but in the end, I'm always reminded that things will work out. Writing has helped me purge my thoughts and feelings. I've been asking for a sign, a clue of what to do, where to go. And the answer is to have faith, believe that all is well, and write. That's the short version, but that was my realization today. I've been called to do great things, and I've been blessed with the right people to help me do them. Two of the greatest things I'll ever do are to love and be with you. You are such a great teacher and mirror. Thanks for doing your job so well!

Longing for you,

Your Reine

July 14, 2014—7:34 p.m.
Day 6

Dearest Roi,

It is challenging at times to weather unpredictable circumstances. It has always taken an extra part of me to give in to emotions that make me feel vulnerable. Love me still, hold me still, and hear me still. I will do this for you in return. I'm confused, but my faith is much stronger than that. Our bond and partnership are stronger than that. I love you now and forever thank you for being who you are.

Loving you always,

La Reine

July 15, 2014—6:49 p.m.
Day 7

My sweet Roi,

I am over the moon with joy. I have something tangible that is mine to show for Reine + Rebelle. Without you, who knows where I would've been in this process? This is a victory for us both—the start of something beautiful. Thank you for pushing and believing. You have and continue to be everything I never knew I needed. I love you!

Forever and always,
La Reine

July 16, 2014—6:30 p.m.
Day 8

Serene Solitude

I went to bed last night with a guided-visualization meditation for depression and woke up feeling energized and renewed. I have realized I need to allow myself to feel my feelings as they come to live a happy life. Not labeling my feelings as good or bad, just choosing to feel them as they come. I may have a job; I have a virtual interview tomorrow. I won't pass this up. My lesson for today is taking things as they come. I wanted to go to homeroom tonight in Miami, but I decided to stay home and reflect. I also applied for jobs. I'm feeling like I'm at the end of this stage I've been caught up in. It feels good.

Love always,
La Reine

July 17, 2014
Day 9

Self-Reflection

Today I woke up feeling challenged and slightly disappointed. I figure, in conclusion, that I just want to make a more conscious effort to be kind. I thought I'd been doing a good job of doing so unconsciously. I don't know; this is where I begin to feel conflicted. It is always my intention to be kind. Sometimes, things get lost in translation. And sometimes you can be the kindest person, but there will be someone who says you do or are the opposite. I think the lesson is to live my truth even if someone else sees it as a lie. This is something that will definitely take time.

Always growing and learning,
La Reine

July 18, 2014—6:33 p.m.
Day 10

Sincere Apology

Dearest Roi,

I woke up this morning with a completely different mind-set. My heart felt free. I'm so thankful for the support and love you give. Thank you for doing the work with me. Thank you for rolling up your sleeves instead of completely walking away when emotions are running high. We are an awesome pair; thank you for always reminding me of this. I love you. I apologize for mentioning breaking up; it's not what I want. I won't do it anymore, because that gets to you, and it's not positive. I want to protect and nurture your heart, not break it. Sharing our lives together, it is my job to hold your heart dear.

Loving you infinitely,

La Reine

July 19, 2014—5:51 p.m.
Day 11

Learning and Growing

My dearest Roi,

The lessons I'm learning are profound. I've had so many aha moments in this time of self-reflection; it's amazing. The reason I love to connect with people is because for so long I felt detached, disconnected, and isolated from the world when I let my deepest, darkest secret consume me. My freedom is so important to me, because I felt enslaved for so many years of keeping this to myself. I understand now why feeling these feelings gets to me. I become that helpless little girl again, searching for someone, anyone, to acknowledge me. Searching for anyone to connect with. Those shackles were an illusion that I have freed myself from. It feels sooooo good to regain my power, to know why I am the way I am. I forgave my father's spirit years ago for the wounds he left behind, but I am finally attentive and mending them. This is tremendous in my growth. Self-coaching is very tough, but the breakthroughs I have are substantial, and they help me be a better partner. I'm so happy about this today; thank you for supporting me in my self-progression.

I love you forever more,
La Reine

August 12, 2014—9:01 p.m.

All my life I've wanted to be free
to grow like a field of sunflowers, tall and wildly.
Wake up smiling with the sun,
and kiss the moon good night.
In life's darkest depths,
I perfect the art of always finding my inner light.
Have a love like air,
like faith,
sustaining and true,
without the need of any proof.
I wasn't born with a wild, beating heart
just to cage love within.
There is beauty in divine multiplication.
Sharing the love and light in me
awakens, sparks, and speaks to that which resides in you.

August 13, 2014—5:08 p.m.

You're funny, kind, and beautiful.
I can't help but feel terrible.
How can I still harbor love in my heart for someone else?
Someone who treats me like less than I am?
I am Queen, and you address me as such,
with no worries about whether the world is big enough
for both of our egos to exist.

August 13, 2014—5:11 p.m.

I have to remember to write
not for shows
or any book I'm trying to compose
but to remind me of my light,
remind me of a girl in love with pouring her heart on paper with pen.
Reading words that seem to be
pieced together to make the most beautiful dream.
A girl that's mixed up,
wondering why simple sentences
turn into the most incomprehensible messages
and numbers like to rearrange their order
on her homework as some kind of torture.
A girl who tries her hardest,
even if it means doing one equation a hundred times
just to make sure her mind isn't playing tricks on her.
She just gets mixed up.
Like on the day her mother got her out of bed
and said her monster,
I mean, father, was dead.
She didn't know whether to cry
or look at it as luck.
Opting not to shed tears in shock,
finally free,
not knowing about the shackles that were left behind mentally.
He drowned, his body somewhere at the bottom of the ocean along
with the key.
But see, she was mixed up.
A thirst for knowledge,
but grades that couldn't get her into an exceptional college
She had so many dreams,
but she loved so many things
that let her down in return.

September 10, 2014—6:45 p.m.

My loving Roi,

I can feel my wings. Even though I'm bound to gravity, in this moment, I feel like I'm flying. Angels sing joyously in my heart, because I'm finally getting hip to God's essence inside me, which has been at my core from the start.

Love,
La Reine

July 18, 2015—10:33 p.m.

Kindness brings us all together.
Humans must learn to use their minds
to get to the end of time
together.
We shall weather the storms
of social norms falling by the wayside.
Pride will no longer have room to consume us,
because we'll have the knowledge of the truest self.
Love will sustain us
when it's all over and done.

July 29, 2015—8:28 p.m.

Love,
I can feel your energy,
feel the core of your being.
It's beautiful; you should share that more with the world.
Something keeps you from revealing just the smallest parts of yourself.
You love to distract yourself with constantly having a new conquest.
Look inside of you; there is nothing on the outside that you need to pursue.

Thank you for the mirror; I see the lesson.
Love and light to you, Will.

October 4, 2015—10:14 p.m.

Soar

Beauty,
you held me in your grips
as soon as my feet touched solid ground.
My heart found a safe place nestled in your bosom.
You reminded me that I am home,
welcomed me with open arms, and it was divine.
From the beginning, I knew in this time spent exploring you
I'd be reintroduced to myself—alone, but then again, never alone.
This was a time to venture deeply,
dive more into me.
I am forever changed.
Though street signs, and
smiling faces appear different; it is all the same.
Thousands of miles away from home,
on my own,
but I feel everyone I love dearly inside of me,
also taking this journey.
They have grown from this experience too,
and it is all thanks to you.
Well, me, I think.
Thank you for taking my hand
and being the first to witness
this next level of my evolution.
For cradling me,
for pushing me past limits
that felt as comfortable as fine linen.
Never knew how to use my wings,
so I've always admired the sky.
Thank you for reminding me I was built to fly.

October 8, 2015—3:02 p.m.

Welcoming the change;
the land is the same.
Time has passed.
My body has grown older, but my soul remains young.
Loving embraces paired with smiling faces
have my heart feeling full.
When we were separated by thousands of miles physically,
from your spirit to mine, every day I'd feel a pull.
Connections that defy space and time
and memories locked in my mind
have helped me get through this time.

October 28, 2015—2:01 p.m.

Dear sixteen-year-old me,

Love is real. No matter how deeply wounded you think you are, you'll be healed. Yes, by your own hands. You'll actually get to experience having a partner that truly is your best friend. No, you won't have to pretend to have it together or continue to battle the illusion that is peer pressure. You're gorgeous, clever, and brilliant. Yes, someone one day besides you will believe it. Your poetry, which in your mind means nothing, is actually your therapy. Keep at it. Continue to smile your biggest, laugh your loudest, and feel the joys of each moment. Baby girl, you've earned it. Forget about perfect; it's only a myth. The definition of home will become fluid by the minute; like sometimes, it's a good-night kiss.

Love,
JLA

Butterfly in the Reine

November 19, 2015—5:29 p.m.

Isolated magic moments in the presence of your love
kept my heart afloat.
Most days,
you were nowhere in sight,
had me lost without a rescue boat,
cast away.
The connection every time we'd touch—I swore could make you stay,
keep you hooked.
You were unreadable, as though I were illiterate,
although I wrote the book.
Because in my eyes, I was a scholar
that studied your love for sport.
I should have known you weren't interested,
because you never showed support.
What carried me was the way your eyes told the truth.
Every time I looked into them
it was as though I took a swim into your big blue ocean.
But I can't be mad at you.
Everyone knew except me
that I was playing the fool.
In reality, you had as much depth
as a puddle after a few days of rain.
Finding sustainable love in you was nothing more
than a game I had no clue how to play.
A master undefeated, you rejoiced
every time I proceeded to think I could win
whenever we tried the love thing again.
Convinced you'd show me a whole new world,
but instead the rug was pulled from under me.

September 15, 2015

This isn't what you dreamed of,
daydreaming when things were tough.
You knew a better way would come someday,
or at least that's what you prayed.
Forging your own path,
escaping from your past,
they will look at you in awe,
or at least that's what you thought.
The wild rose that grew from concrete,
she rose above the adversity.
The baby bird with a broken wing
is now full grown and soaring.
You never thought you'd live a life that was boring.
The spirit of a gypsy,
ready for a lifetime of exploring,
'til the day he came along,
his smile and words adoring.
The way you walked, as though your feet kissed the earth with each step—an exotic creature you were that brought on feelings he never felt.
His admiration turned into obsession, but you couldn't tell.
His pretty words had you under his spell,
so in love with him you fell.

March 29, 2016—9:45 p.m.

Fear of the Free Fall

Desires of freedom occupy my mind,
directly from my heart.
My logic comes up
with a million reasons why
it isn't right.
But at last,
I have faced my fear of flying,
of soaring to startling heights,
of experiencing depths of life
I never knew could be true.
Along come you,
disguised as ordinary.
You disarmed me with sincerity.
Your vulnerability
taught me the gift of visibility,
the power in baring my naked soul to finally feel free
in love.
Feel the truth of genuine trust
to be liberated in living life fully,
being exactly who it is I want to be.
Your love for me
reminds me daily that I am whimsically exquisite,
that my existence is beautifully ironic.
Your love is magic.
Realizing how irrational fear of the leap is,
I've been reminded that I have wings.
Free.

April 5, 2016—10:17 p.m.

Smiling to the heavens
doesn't mean that I'm forgetting to plant my feet on the ground.
I'm basking in the glory that my transient self-love,
seemingly misplaced, has been found.
I don't forget how it feels to be at the bottom of the pit.
I stand despite it,
rise tall—humbled and wise.
Every crisis has a lesson that turns out to be a prize,
reasons why I must comply and trust life's journey.
Remember that I'll never be given more than I can handle;
remember not to be detoured by adversity;
remember how strong my mother raised me to be.

May 21-22, 2016—10 p.m.

My life's purpose is to love you,
nurture you,
grow you.
When I hold you,
eyes closed,
then look up
and my arms are wrapped around the whole world,
I look at your reflection, mesmerized.
Your scars tell stories
that could have ended without you standing before me.
At times, I feel unworthy
to be graced by your enormous, wondrous presence.
You smile, and I am intoxicated by your essence.
Wisdom from your ancestors makes your soul hum.
You journey,
moment by moment,
through this life supported by the thousands who came before you,
disguised as though you are alone.
Earth,
woman,
you are my universe.
Even through the darkest depths,
I'll always put you first.
Your features resemble your father
stitched together carefully with the eyes of your mother,
a place their love can exist in harmony.
All that has transpired is for the greater good.

Letters to La Reine

Sunshine,

Defy your strongest doubts and smile as big as you can muster, even if your heart isn't in it or you feel foolish. Close your eyes, and kiss the sky. Thank it for its unwavering beauty, the way the moon lights the darkest of nights. The clouds gather for rain, bringing nourishment to the earth, just as with your soul after you've shed tears when you hurt. I know it may sound strange, but everything has its purpose. The peaks and valleys exist simultaneously.
Love always,
JLA

iii

May 30, 2016—9:37 p.m.

You don't owe me anything.
You're so good at reminding me of this fact.
I wonder when you'll tire of hoarding your true feelings,
exhaust yourself of playing life like a game of poker.
Your face never gives you away.
When will you realize no one else wants to play?
You holding cards close to your chest is
all there is.
Staring at your reflection in the mirror,
what is it that you truly fear?
Waking up to mounds of discarded emotions?
That you'll drown in them as though you were in the big blue ocean?
Instead of going against the current,
let it take you over.
This is the only way to get through
the inevitable end.

June 4, 2016—9:56 a.m.

"Be silent.
Tell no one," he says.
I became envious of those cursed by being mute,
words banned from leaving their lips.
How deeply I wanted this!
Then I wouldn't have to pretend
or have to weave together monologues,
entertaining a facade of normalcy,
as though I wasn't hurting,
like my sky was not falling.
"Be quiet," she said.
"Dry your eyes; take it like a woman, and do not cry."
Puzzled,
wondering how I'm supposed to hide
the hurricane occurring inside me,
how I'll avoid drowning internally.
"You can't hold water," they say.
They are unaware that this isn't what water was meant for,
so incognizant of the power of the outpour.
Overcoming my own ignorance of this
has liberated my life experience.
Now I am increasingly met with confusion
when others discover my rebellion against confinement,
of silence.
If you do not tell the truth about your pain,
leave it up to them,
and they'll say
you delighted in it all.

June 4, 2016—11:16 p.m.

Is this love that I'm feeling?
Is it normal to be indifferent
for moments, hours, days?
Fighting you for the greater good of our love,
misplaced it as we debated who was right for the trillionth time.
Where is it?
It must be somewhere in this pile of insults we've thrown to one-up
each other.

Butterfly in the Reine
June 16, 2016—11:55 a.m.

Nothing romantic about the moment.
Naked,
but
I had a change in heart.
You refused to accept my words.
Your hand stopped my voice,
my breath,
from ending things.
Choking
showed me I had no power
over my body.
The rain surrounding us
poured down violently.
Inside, I'm screaming.
In the distance, the ocean waves
crashing,
taking the place of the tears.
Fear
I couldn't show on my face.
I have since brought others to my grave,
where you killed me.
None of them seemed to notice my dead body.
So, we walk past like nothing ever happened.
I drive past you like nothing ever happened.
You picked up a hobby of panhandling,
pretending to be homeless
to feed your addiction.
Something you learned in rehab.
People call you crazy.
I never called you crazy.
Is that crazy?
A thousand miles from home,
I am alone.
Speeding on the way to my destination,
I see red and blue lights in my rear view,
no sirens.
I am silent.
He speaks politely,
asks for my information,
and I comply.

Butterfly in the Reine

He hands me my ticket with my identification.
I finally release my prolonged exhalation.
This is when the storm takes over me.
I begin crying,
hyperventilating uncontrollably,
remembering the last time I was violated
by someone who was hired to protect me.
He wore a uniform too,
although the rage in his eyes
wasn't supposed to be a part of the suit.
I remember attempting to defend
my right to police the treatment of my body.
Instead, I am choked once again,
to be reminded that I have no power.
He made sure I knew that in his eyes I was nobody.
That night yet another part of me died.
More than a year later, far away from that grave site,
I still cry,
trying to stay alive,
trying to behave.
This polite officer says,
"I'm sorry for your experience, but we are not all that way."

July 1, 2016—11:57 p.m.

Remember when I almost let you come inside?
We danced with the notion all night,
braved an angelic city under a starry sky.
I still think of the glow in your smile.
You've always admired the midnight of my skin,
the indigo glow under the moonlight.
We finally had a chance to be alone.
I guess it took us being miles from home.
Finally able to explore your gorgeous mind
with no distractions.
A mutual attraction so palpable,
yet you remain the perfect gentleman,
accepting all that I'm willing to divulge.
I trust it'll be a stellar experience
just by the consideration in your touch.
Gentle but wise,
a patient longing in your eyes
each time we hold a gaze.
We both know
untamed desire grows.
Careful consideration must be taken
to avoid being engulfed by the fire we made.
Tired of tiptoeing on hot coals,
I throw salt to end it all,
to save us both the pain that follows the inevitable withdrawal.

July 15, 2016—12:12 a.m.

I bathe in glitter.
There are galaxies that reside within me,
bush full and fruitful.
Skin on my legs mimics the fur of wolves.
I once misunderstood
what it meant to be woman,
ever changing,
always becoming.
The moment I think I crack the code of who I am,
things change.
A game that never gets old.
The day I began to menstruate
I thought would be the end of my fate.
But that was only the beginning of
periodically shedding versions of me that are no longer fitting.

July 15, 2016—10:09 p.m.

Meet me at the Eiffel Tower
twenty years from now
so we can officially
French kiss.
Like in our early twenties,
we got so much practice.
Remember the parking garage after our first date?
We made out for three hours straight.
Well, in pretty much every parking lot, anyway.
We didn't yet have homes of our own,
so we found shelter in each other.
Today I mourn you,
because I cannot ignore
your absence any longer.
I can't bear the thought
of never seeing you again,
touching you again.
Besides anything else,
you were my friend.
I never expected a day would come when you were not.
I know we couldn't work in the romantic sense long term.
This poem,
this book,
is the end of it all.
It's sad that we're dead to each other.
I always wanted to meet your mother;
tell her I said hello.
Give her a hug from a girl she'll never know,
a girl who always fantasized
of bearing children with her son's eyes.
You protected me from everyone but you;
sometimes that meant shielding me from myself.

July 18, 2016—3:21 p.m.

I am born from people who knew how to free themselves.
Their spirits live inside me.
On my best
and especially worst days,
my ancestors push me.
Remind me that I have been passed the baton.
Reassure me that my sole existence
means the race is already won.

July 28, 2016—9:59 p.m.

I've always had a thing for beauty.
Forgive me for
falling for your gorgeous,
seeing past all you hide,
past your attempt to wear the lies
you were forced to believe as true
and facades that were mistaken for the real you.
Forgive my ability to see,
sense,
hear,
and speak the truth.
I decided way back
that the life of upholding illusions isn't where it's at.
Forget who they told you to be.
Forget the rules they made up.
Realize that you exist despite them.
Liberate yourself from living someone else's life.
Live the way you want to.
Be a sight for sore eyes.
And the memories you've gained
from the life that you made?
Take them to the grave.
And at your funeral,
all anyone will say is,
"Here lies someone who truly, lived."

July 31, 2016—11:59 p.m., ten minutes

Who could have known that
he'd steal your soul?
Certainly
not me.
I had no clue that
he'd run off with your voice.
Did not know
it wasn't your choice.
Forgive my deaf ears;
it seems I could not hear
your screaming.
Cast out alone,
with no way home,
I lay in bed blissfully dreaming.
The sun comes up.
I search for you
with no luck.
A call with terrible news
struck my heart,
and suddenly I'm a statue
with no idea of what to do.
Torn apart because
I wasn't there,
didn't understand.
And now
your blood is on my hands.

August 3, 2016—6:24 p.m.

I talk to you the way I talk to me.
Isn't that the sweetest thing?
Except, of course,
love isn't forceful in her delivery.
You're constantly forgiving me,
because I discard the Handle with Care signs
stamped all over you.
Too old to blame Mommy;
Daddy's been dead.
So instead,
I'll acknowledge that I need help
learning how to love.

August 7, 2016—11:50 p.m.

Thanks for the memories
that became poetry—for the heartbreak,
even though
it wasn't so great.

August 11, 2016—10:00 p.m.

Sitting in the clouds,
thoughts of you are just as loud.
Logic escapes me.
Clutching my rose quartz pendant,
because memories have my heart in a choke hold.
Visions projected on the inside of my eyelids
without my permission.
A single tear falls,
hits the ground,
breaking like glass.
Watching you bowing before her
on one knee
reminds me of how fragile
I still am.

August 11, 2016—10:15 p.m.

I sit in the heartbreak you gifted.
It's the only part of you left
to keep me company.
Time has come and gone.
We both have love that is going strong.
But, sometimes, over a glass of wine,
I dress up in the mess we made,
pretend there was an alternate end.
Like I succeeded in being this woman
who was not only pretty to look at
but had few demands
and fewer opinions.
Got along with all of your friends,
came from a well-to-do family,
so your mother would definitely like me.
And your dad would pat you on the back,
in approval,
saying you got a good one.

August 12, 2016—8:38 p.m.

My journal is a cemetery
where all my half-finished love poems lay to rest.
I could never grasp the realities of love's physicalities, I guess.
I could only ever understand love in theory.
Maybe that is why hearts turn to stone whenever they come near me,
leaving sunflowers for the ghosts of lovers past.
Thanks for the memories—they're the only things that last.
They say the only true love
is self-love.
I'm loving myself
through losing the world.

August 13, 2016—2:53 p.m.

I've been selfless;
I've been selfish.
Both seem to fit well.
I'm committed
to authenticity.
I've been an angel;
I've seen the devil
a few times
in my own eyes.
With no regret,
I admit
that it felt good
to be bad.
I'm sure this comes as no surprise.
I was heartless.
I was reckless,
wore my pride
as a necklace,
both boldly
and ever so proudly.

August 24, 2016—1:20 p.m.

Let my people go.
If I should die before they wake,
I pray they know my soul
was never theirs to take.
Our light will ultimately cast out their darkness.

August 25, 2016—midnight

I was born
with lips sewed shut.
Born girl,
just another waste of space
in this patriarchal world.
My mother learned invisibility from my grandmother,
who learned it from her mother,
who learned it from hers.
I bet if I go far enough back,
I'll find the first woman who was silenced for existing,
bred to be nothing more but
a well for the world.
Nourish those who bled us dry.
Because without being slave;
or servant.
Without women, this world can't survive.
So, if we are all-powerful,
why are we convinced,
misled, to believe false truths?

iv

October 13, 2016—8:41 p.m.

Somewhere I began to shrink
for fear of being intimidating,
too grand.
So, I made myself more vanilla.

October 27, 2016—2:35 a.m.

California was a dream.
Every day, sunshine;
never a single cloud in the sky.
On my return home;
Tombstone.
Hurricane threatens destruction,
only to leave behind heavy rain
and gloomy skies,
reigniting my love
for the beauty of clouds.
On those California days,
all I did was beg for rain—
so I could be reminded of home.
Most days I have a handle
on this internal battle.
Most days I feel fine.
This morning I had to physically walk away
from a group of police officers
to prove that I could,
to prove I was free,
to prove that my life belongs to me.
Young girl, go ahead and cry.
Grieve your traumas.
Don't you dare be in a rush to dry your eyes.
Take as long as you need.
Just remember one thing:
it has been you
present for every moment that has passed by.
So, when you look into your own eyes
at your savior,
don't you dare forget to smile
and say thank you.
3:20 a.m.

October 27, 2016—1:49 p.m.

Spirit gives me
visions of treasure.
I wake with the taste
of abundance on my tongue.
Obstacles attempt to distract from
my mission.
The road gets lonely;
thirst and hunger seem to overtake me;
the desire to relieve my quench for purpose
surfaces while feeling starved for direction and support.
I cry a river and save myself.

October 16, 2016—1:38 p.m.

How dare you be flawed
and expect me to love selflessly!
How dare you stumble and fall
and then tell me you need me!
How dare I allow tears to trickle from my eyes,
to feel empathy,
when all I've ever relied on was me,
when I've brought myself back from death
several times
without your help,
without your consideration.
What I'm saying
is that I've lost the patience
to be expected to fix your life for you.
I know it is my fault that you've been spoiled.
How could I have a change of heart after all this time?
As a human being,
I reserve the right to change my mind,
to restructure my boundaries,
even if you are my family.
I must live for me.

October 26, 2016—2:04 p.m.

I have come to terms with the fact
that I'll never stop writing about you.
Your essence will be a thread in all that I do.
My palms ached in anticipation
of contacting your skin.
I've done rituals to cut the energetic cords
we were entangled in.
But there are still remnants
left of you in my fingertips.
It's like the love you couldn't outwardly show
and the words you were too prideful to let me know
were gifted in the form of bittersweet poetry.
I am reminded that energy cannot be destroyed,
only transformed.
And it is the only true currency.
This is energetic alchemy.
These poems are the flowers you never gave me.
I've given birth to this book
instead of your baby.
As much as I cursed your name when you left,
without the heartbreak you handed me,
this masterpiece could never be.
I see the blessing in it all.

October 30, 2016—11:46 p.m.

I've inherited a flawed world,
journeying in a flawed body
created by two
who never knew
that in the flaws lie beauty.
I can feel the lessons
for many generations
down my lineage.
I've always felt the responsibility to be
who they were too afraid to be.
To go to places they could only pray to see.
I'm abundant with the energy my ancestors saved
from not being allowed to live their way,
playing a lifelong game of ordinary.
No one ever told them
about the treasures in their chest.
No one told them that with heart,
you can have and do anything.
I know my world belongs to me.
I know that this body is my home
and also the house of God.

November 15, 2016—6:13 p.m.

I want to tell her to breathe.
But that is the worst thing to do when drowning.
I want to say, "Open your eyes."
But she is afraid of her demise.
I want to say, "Reach your arms out."
But she cannot hear me,
no matter how loud I shout.
What shall I do?

November 15, 2016—8:33 p.m.

Pebbles feel like boulders.
She's got the whole world on her shoulders,
wishing pride didn't stop the tears from falling from her eyes.

November 18, 2016—3:01 p.m.

Made shelter in the darkness,
waiting for dawn.
Felt the sadness and loneliness tenfold.
I'm not sure what to make of what has become of me.
Don't know how to act
now that the sun is shining.
Peace is tough to embrace
when the war is finally over.

Butterfly in the Reine

December 2, 2016—9:45 a.m.

The sound of symphonies
drew you here.
The sweet voice of
Ella Fitzgerald wailing
made you climb the crystal staircase
for a taste,
hopeful to touch the beauty that is me.
You've knocked
now at my feet,
begging to enter my sanctuary,
admiring the regality of it all—this life that I've made,
dragons I've slain,
victories
I've claimed.
I won't dare discard
the crown I've rightfully earned,
and exchange it,
for your love.
I've come to my own rescue
from myself
and the obstacles that have tried to claim my life.
Finally formed an alliance with
my darkness
and light.
I'm who I've been waiting for
my entire life.
You have no power here.

December 6, 2016—2:15 p.m.

Zann,
I miss you, dearly.
Our hugs,
pikliz attitude,
and the smiles we'd share.
Whenever I come to visit,
I knock and no one is there.
Except,
on occasion,
when I feel like I've braved the darkest forests,
I make it to you,
and there you are
with open arms,
smiling and laughing just the way I love.
I wrote poems for you;
I wrote down my story
for the day I get too tired to remember,
too tired of swallowing
all that has happened to me,
for the day the cat catches my tongue,
and I decide I'm too tired to recognize anyone,
tired of being disappointed in the story's ending.
For the day I free myself from pretending
to have it all together.
On these pages I can be vulnerable,
and it isn't unbearable for me
or those reading,
if anyone besides me cares to read one day.
I dedicate this to my grandmother—
my favorite firecracker.

December 7, 2016—12:22 a.m.

I know she's nice,
but I bet she don't have the sauce you need.
Too Switzerland,
always on the fence,
too tamed.
Too safe,
when you're used to flames.

December 9, 2016—3:04 p.m.

Waiting up for you,
the bouquet of sunflowers has wilted,
dead.
I've started to forget some of the words you said.
Looking for you in all the places we went;
faintly remember the sound of your voice.
Sent smoke signals,
but for some reason,
you still won't come.

December 9, 2016—4:56 p.m.

Maybe it was too much to bare
to feel ten times the amount of fear
you instilled in so many
all at once.
Exiled from both lands,
your skeleton destined for
the bottom of the ocean.
Burning bridges
with no consequences
might have given you
a sense of fearlessness—superhero complex.
Karma can be so humbling.
Brought you back to earth.
You're just a mortal being
who must pay for his mistakes.

December 10, 2016—1:15 p.m.

The more I move despite fear,
the more the world opens up for me,
the sea parts to make way for me.
Angels push me,
carry me through.
They rejoice;
they've been waiting for me
to wake up all along
and shed this cloak of ordinary.

December 13, 2016—2:53 p.m.

Sister,
watching you blossom brings me joy.
Brothers,
cheering you on has been my
part-time job since you were little boys.
Mother,
letting go of the picture
you had in your head for my life set me free.
Auntie,
your emphasis on scholastic achievement
help me find my unconventional genius.

December 20, 2016—2:15 p.m.

Sandi,
some days I can't stop crying.
Some days I feel like a zombie,
a ghost.
Some days I can still feel the chokes.
The scene is on constant loop.
Sandi, I could have been you.
I feel ashamed when I am weak,
when I can barely breathe.
Sandi,
I know you are here.
I try to survive through the fear;
no one understands.
Some days, I don't.
I saw him, and I wanted to hide,
fearing that I'd be a threat once again in his eyes.
I've written letters to him,
burned them,
and prayed to be released from it all.
Fear is what he wanted;
fear is what I've been left with.
I begged to see the lesson,
to find the blessing in my loss that night.
All I have is my story.
I am afraid to fight;
fighting for myself nearly got me killed.
Sandi, when will this country be healed?
All I have is my story,
so I shall speak.
For when I am dead,
they will know where I stand
on this country's epidemic.

December 21, 2016—6:54 p.m.

So I didn't pass the test.
Tears too tired to keep falling.
Don't want to continue to break my own heart trying
to convince you that my flaws are worth loving,
worth accepting,
that my good traits aren't sold separately.
Never wanted to be owned.
Maybe that's where I went wrong.
In my mind, love isn't possession.
Maybe I gave the wrong impression—me not needing you.
Doesn't mean you aren't desired,
that our relationship isn't a vital part of my life.

December 26, 2016—7:26 p.m.

All our lives,
we are trying to break open a treasure chest.
Many tire and bore quickly of the frustration.
Few persist and are introduced to their own light.
I've been afraid of it all along,
but I've learned to love and move past my fear.
Amen.

January 7, 2017—8:15 p.m.

In the beginning,
I thought you were interesting.
You loved to listen to scores from your favorite movies.
In the end, you said, "Jenn, this isn't a movie."
Ruined all of your things,
so you could see what your betrayal did to me.
Somehow afterward I still felt empty.
You stand tall,
while I'm wishing you'd crumble
for me to witness.
It isn't fair that I'm a mess,
and you're the blame.
Disappointed that this has become our reality.

January 8, 2017—11:06 p.m.

I shine my light bright.
Cover your eyes if you can't stand it.
The more I wake up to who I am,
false fits
fall away.
In the past, my tears created rivers.
Present day,
I bow
and trust the universe
has a better way.

January 9, 2017—11:20 a.m.

Thank you
for love,
for life
through words
in moments
of silence,
and an array of emotions.
During a story,
I could never predict,
only live to tell,
never forgetting the start.
The first time I thought of the end,
my escape became
paper and pen.

January 10, 2017—2:00 p.m.

Things to consider during the storm:
when the dust finally settles,
when silence is peace,
no longer chaos
as you once perceived.
Realize the rain is necessary
to baptize your pain,
to purify your heart
when the sun rises again.

January 15, 2017—12:33 p.m.

When was the last time someone asked how you're really doing?
Beyond just surviving,
how does your heart feel?
I see you shrinking,
shriveling up inside of your shell,
getting your to-dos checked off of your lists.
Has no one ever told you that life is more than this,
more than waking up to yesterday's unfinished tasks
springing you out of bed?
There is so much more than that going on in your head.
The human mind and body are beautiful things
that weren't made as machines
to just do.
It's okay
to just be.
No one is coming to punish you for existing.
You are free.
I, too, know the fear of going within,
being fearful to explore emotions.
Dive deep;
over 70 percent of you is made up of water.
You are the sea.

January 22, 2017—2:14 p.m.

Dry eyes;
every woman in me is drowning.
This pain isn't new.
I hear whispers,
clairaudiently:
"Who said it couldn't happen to you?"
We've been served betrayal for generations,
like food.
We are all
still starving
but not waiting,
because the world keeps spinning.

January 24, 2017—7:55 a.m.

Dream Insights

Adulthood is about intentionally being in integrity
as consistently as possible.
I've never seriously dated a grown adult male—just young men
wearing shoes too big,
hoping to one day grow into them,
trying to figure life out.
That type of guy is too juvenile for my current lifestyle.
My needs and wants have changed.
I don't want a boy trying to figure out the world, himself, and how a
woman fits into his life;
I want a man who has become wise from his triumphs and mistakes
and uses the knowledge gained as a compass to navigate through life.

January 31, 2017—3:55 a.m.

I bleed openly,
not ashamed,
unafraid,
proud
to be washed anew,
beautiful,
shedding the walls
of darkness,
long dead,
lessons gained,
earned,
more valuable
than any amount of currency imaginable.
I don't blame you for being baffled.
I would be too,
if I were you.
This inner-standing was overdue.
Reine,
woman,
mirror,
world.
You are incredible.
4:08 a.m.

February 10, 2017—2:40 p.m.

I hope you're reading this
on a gorgeous day,
soaking up the sun's rays,
being present for yourself, and
smiling, because it'll always be you
and no one else
that gets to see
the masterpiece
created
from beginning to end.
I hope you marvel
at what God made
with your help.
You are phenomenal.

February 10, 2017—3:18 p.m.

Living with PTSD,
fear is a tab that stays open
against my will.
At times, I manage to minimize
this window.
I never know
what will force it back open.
Uniformed servicemen?
Being alone in an unfamiliar building?
I don't know the exits;
where are the exits?
When I am among a sea of strangers
with smiling faces,
can they be trusted?
If there is an uproar,
can I escape?
Will I be trampled as
they seek safety?
Fair-skinned ladies watch as I
buy groceries.
Do they find me threatening?
When they speak to me,
is my response polite enough?
Will they call for me to be removed?
Is the audacity of my presence/existence
in their safe space
considered rude?

February 13, 2017—5:34 p.m.

I cannot trust a man who doesn't believe in love.
It means
he doesn't believe in himself.
What shall I do with that?
For if you do not believe in love,
nothing is safe,
no place is sacred.
I cannot unpack myself.
My treasures are at risk of being stolen.
A man who doesn't believe in love
will try and steal all I have for his own,
unaware of the riches housed by his rib cage.
My dear,
you must believe in love.
It is, in fact,
what you are made of.
Don't let this world convince you otherwise.

February 13, 2017—9:24 p.m.

Turn the TV off;
It's got you thinking you're a savage
in the jungle
trying to survive
in a dog-eat-dog world.
Look in the mirror.
You've been begging to be seen.
Look yourself in the eyes.
Deep inside,
there is a glorious light that
no savage could humble himself enough to notice.
Stay focused
in this concrete jungle.
It'd be a shame if you lost yourself
trying to be liked by someone else
who doesn't even know himself.

February 18, 2017—3:33 p.m.

I remember I wished that God could make me
as beautiful as Vanessa Williams.
Mesmerized by those green eyes
staring back at me on that magazine cover.
Her skin was so fair,
in awe of her flowing hair.
This must be what God considers beauty.
My mama doesn't look like me,
or herself anymore.
My sister came out looking like a stranger.
Mama asked the doctor what she was—a good, chunky baby,
black as the night without stars.
If you were ignorant,
you'd mock that type of gorgeous by calling it tar.
God made my sister beautiful;
she grew up to be my mother's mirror.
Sometimes I wonder if it's eerie?
Maybe it's a relief
that my sister looks at her reflection
and wouldn't want to change a thing.

February 18, 2017—4:18 p.m.

They try and convince me that freedom is a fantasy.
But freedom is a legacy passed on to me.
Freedom is my destiny.
No one can ever take that away.

March 2, 2017—10:30 a.m.

I miss you,
but I haven't even held you yet.
You've grown beautifully.
You're curious about the world
beyond the walls of what I have taught.
You want to go places I've never been.
You beg, say only good can come from it,
for us to share the experience of newness.
Hearts will be gorgeously
stretched by adventure.
Will the world be as kind,
considerate,
and patient as I have?
Will they make you question yourself,
since they do not understand your brilliance?
Will you be easily influenced,
eager to change
to fit into society's frame of perfection?
I guess I am afraid of
how you'll react encountering rejection.
There is nothing I can do to ease the sting.
I wonder about the places you'll find yourself,
the people you'll meet,
the conversations you'll have, and
the impression you'll leave.
I wonder if,
through your exploration,
you'll find peace.
I can't wait to hear the stories you'll tell,
the emotions you've felt.
I hope you are proud of where you are from.
You are what has been made from love and lessons,
what was created once I let go of expectation.
I've been fearful of you leaping and ultimately falling.
I only ever wanted to see you fly.

March 8, 2017—10:10 p.m.

We are the gods;
we are the wise ancestors.
We are history.
My art is already a
critically acclaimed masterpiece.
All is one,
past and future;
both exist in the present.
In this moment, I am home.
Here is where I live.
My life unfolds according
to my next move.

Butterfly in the Reine
March 9, 2017—11:48 a.m.

I didn't want to write this.
I didn't want to give this any fuel.
I've repeated it to myself
like a hundred Hail Mary's.
Still, I have not been freed.
I forgive you,
I forgive me.
Pain has invaded my veins;
I claw at my skin.
I feel it pulsating.
I've fought tirelessly against tears
too hot to fall;
a fire could start.
I refuse to risk falling apart
due to your betrayal.
I forgive you,
I forgive me.
This wouldn't have happened
if I hadn't let you come so close,
if I hadn't given you a key.
Your resentment was palpable;
how could I be surprised?
When I displayed love for myself,
I saw the envy in your eyes.
How could I not see it coming?
I forgive you,
I forgive me.
As much as this hurts,
I'd die a million times
if I were to commit such a crime.
I'll move on from this eventually.
Your behavior is a result of a cancer
condoning such a reckless mentality.
I forgive you,
I forgive me.
I forgive you,
I forgive me.
I forgive you,
I forgive me.
I forgive you,

Butterfly in the Reine
I forgive me.
I forgive you,
I forgive me.
I forgive you,
I forgive me.
I forgive you,
I forgive me.
I forgive you,
I forgive me.
I forgive you,
I forgive me.
Amen.

March 9, 2017—1:44 p.m.

Dear Love,
I am writing you to find out who convinced you that you are not a king. You say you have no kingdom, but I know you don't believe this. This world has let you down plenty, and I understand your cynicism. Do not forget who you are, love. Do not diminish yourself. If you knew what God intended for the cells dancing inside you, your perspective would change. Who taught you that being soft is a weakness? Why do you hate that some refer to your daughter as a princess? She ought to be taught her value early. You of all people know that if you aren't careful, her confidence can be robbed by society. You are a king, but I know sometimes it doesn't feel that way. Listen to your heart, your kingdom, and answers are there.

In spirit,
Jenn La Reine

March 12, 2017—11:06 p.m.

Judgment won't get you
to the other side
of yourself
or them.
Judgment isn't the path
to experience peace.

March 13, 2017—4:59 p.m.

I write to keep from drowning.
Writing is swimming,
maneuvering through the depths of my soul.
This earth is so vast,
with many demands
that will take you under if you wander.
Writing is my life jacket,
my only productive attachment.

March 20, 2017—4:40 p.m.

Little girl,
whose life are you living?
You thought it would always be sweet?
That honey would drip endlessly
from the corner of your lips?
Duality is real.
By now, you should be acquainted.
You don't remember missing the rain
when the sun shone too much?
You've forgotten the times you sought out shade
when the sunshine wanted to love you up.
You know the rain makes the leaves your favorite hue of green.
There is a purpose for everything.
Humble yourself.

Butterfly in the Reine
March 23, 2017—8:04 p.m.

Venus rotates backward.
Life and I are in a different chapter.
You spring in my mind,
the season before summertime.
Four years ago,
I let you go,
set us free.
I always knew you'd remain a part of me.
I think of you when I'm doing things
I told you I could only dream of.
I hope one day you get to see that
the heartbreak wasn't the most important part of what we had.
You spoke life into me;
that's a fact.
I try and find you
in the places we've been
as young adults,
deep down just
grown-ass kids.
I know you're happy.
So am I, overall.
I still have hope that we'll link up
and have a good chuckle
at the happenings of those days.
I still remember your gaze.
I thought it was love in your eyes.
Maybe it was.
Now I know
you saw something magical
when I was too busy
trying to describe the light I saw in you,
like undiscovered galaxies.
I'd explain how wonderful you are.
You'd blush and respond,
"You flatter me."
It wasn't flattery,
just what you needed to know.
I hope my watering words
somehow helped you grow.

March 25th, 2017—6:20 p.m.

I admire those who have loved and lost
and loved again.
The way I have come to know you is so intimate.
I know your quirks,
strengths, and weaknesses so fondly.
Our closeness is astounding,
terrifying at times.
I know you well.
I'm under your spell.
Why would I want anything different?
You're so familiar to me.

March 26th, 2017—11:34 a.m.

Heartbreak tried to take my light away.
Disease tried to take my smile away.
Betrayal tried to kill my belief in honesty.
Insecurity tried to bury me alive.
I didn't die
but clawed my way out of the grave,
laughing loudly,
exposing every tooth in my crooked smile,
wishing fortune, love, and light
for the ones who thought I'd drown in the darkness.
Naked,
unashamed,
don't care about
what they could say.
Beaming,
my light bringing death to all the demons.
They have no place here.

March 31, 2017—10:15 a.m.

There is nothing romantic about suffering.
Who said poetry is the same as fairy tales?
Curiosity killed the cat
and the little girl
who wondered '*what Langston
could be getting at?*'
Yes, she pondered.
'*What happens to a dream deferred?*'
She unknowingly embarked
on a lifelong hunt, to solve this riddle.
Later, Lorraine demonstrated the cause and effect
of a raisin in the sun.
Still,
the little girl never imagined that
perhaps she could become one of them
or that art could imitate life.
How eerie it was to wake up
and realize she'd be writing
the same poem,
the same story!
It isn't beautiful
to live unfulfilled.
Swallowing potential
can eat away at a person's insides.
You've seen the undead
walking among you.
Although spirit is housed
in these rented bodies,
the magic it possesses
was not meant to be contained.
I'm writing a story
not new but
all my own—a tale of the
darkness,
death,
and rebirth
the caterpillar
endures in the cocoon.

Butterfly in the Reine

From ordinary
to butterfly destiny.
Those who come after me will know that
life ain't no crystal stair.
This journey has no map,
no manual.
No one can walk this path for you.
There are few that share the flowers
that beg for permission to bloom from their tired heads.
This is my experiment to see what happens
when I gift this earth my precious
sunflowers and daisies.
Every moment I've lived
grew them into something flawed
and beautiful.
I'm as proud as anyone
who has ever lived
could ever be.
Free.

Teach your light.

Printed in Great Britain
by Amazon